LIFETAKER

BILL SHIELDS

©1995 2.13.61 Publications

FIRST PRINTING

ISBN # 1-880985-30-6

Cover painting: **Peter Cunis**

Edit: **H**

Design: **▬**

D0869932

2.13.61

P.O. BOX 1910 · LOS ANGELES · CALIFORNIA · 90078 · USA

2.13.61 INFO HOTLINE #: (213)969-8043

This book would not have existed without Henry Rollins, my daughters, a wicked bad marriage and Post Traumatic Stress Disorder

I would not have existed without all the help from my wife, Lisa Shields and my son Rob Yeager

I gave my life for these words

so be it.

1992

no message, no fortune cookie
you don't love anyone,
she was saying,

not me
not yourself

not even your kids

I was sitting in the living room chair watching cable
flicking from channel to channel

I didn't hear a damn word

she pulled the afghan around her body
crying in her own-made world

I agree absolutely
the man is dead inside

I'm exactly what you see

portrait of a man as a young suicide
we sat in my car sipping coffee out a thermos
smoking a cigarette & staring at the river

damn cold outside
I kept the motor running, the heater on

no more point to it
he said

it'll never end

I agreed
lit another cigarette
we had nothing in common but Vietnam
he was six years older & had two more kids

the police found him in his garage a year later
dead at the wheel w/the motor running

a paycheck in his pocket
already signed

a man in the bag
he has a glass eye that tears up
& a picture of himself in Vietnam in his wallet

2 eyes in that picture
a head of hair

Sturge lives w/his parents still
44 years old & sleeps in his teenage bedroom

sells auto parts
occasional cars

always a handgun stuck in his pants
a Kleenex dabbing at that fake eye

never married
completely divorced

we talk a bit
he's never had one nightmare from the war

put it all right behind him
forgotten in a little bag

he'll tell you all about his .30 cal machine gun
that could lead a man in the paddies

when he poured fire out the door of a helicopter
people went face down bloody

& he'll roll a cigarette
look at me w/that one good eye

& say

you know how it was
Bill

Jesus Christ & a few others
the wrong side of midnight
I'm dead in the bed, a blanket over my face

wide awake
w/the chins of long-forgotten people touching my eyes

my mother is back from the grave tonight
my daughter is too

I'm walking back down the streets of Saigon
looking at the bars & sweating badly

next to me a body wiggles
puts my hand in its mouth to keep from screaming

enough

3 hours to work & my ex-wife is pacing in the wings

wanting her turn
on my cross

the alarm clock flashed 12:00 all night

I fall on my knees
head flat on the floor

pure pain
all regrets

pathetic
a 40 year old man

feeling sorry
pitiful for himself

shot & stabbed
in war

shot & stabbed
by himself

in
Pennsylvania

no reinforcements
no helicopters

the medic
killed himself

an hour
ago

I'm on my knees
waiting for a kind word

& just one
reason

in my fortieth winter
3:38 a.m.
tv on

black dead
living room

my wife walks out
of the bedroom

stands in the hallway
& says

what the hell is wrong with you?

she turns around
& in a minute, I hear the bed squeak

I watch the window, the snow falling

like thunder
all night

check list
the winter of '85
an efficiency apartment in Minneapolis

no car/mice/cockroaches/absent landlord

a typewriter
6 pairs of pants

6 shirts
2 pairs of shoes

the stove lit
& the burners on

temperature inside
never above 50 degrees

seeing my breath
as I typed

I fell asleep at night praying
to any god to die

in May
I left

shook the roaches
out of the toaster

wiped the blood
off the walls

& picked .357 shells
out of the carpet

I handed the landlord
my keys
&
a scream

the wave of her hand
I've wanted to say to a woman
don't disappear now

one woman to hold my soul in her hand
& not feel her fingers burn to the bone

stainless tough
w/a soft laugh

no apologies
sitting in the dark bedroom watching the neighbor's headlights

I've thought too much about her
she was so much better

than my marriage
& myself

one woman to carry me on her shoulder
hold the hand of my dead daughter

I don't think you exist
lady

but I'll lie myself
to the grave

w/belief

veterans' rap group
an empty chair next to me
middle-aged men talking all around it

the babble
of defeat

light a cigarette
stare at the wall

thinking of ex-wives
children

bad jobs

& wonder
where it all went wrong

knowing

home
two hours
till tomorrow

no words
tonight

my imagination
has committed suicide

the pain of one man
in a room wishing

he was anywhere
but there

alive
or dead

walls
a little music

I stare
at my hands

then lock
the door

punching the clock, digging the hole

never saw a pair of bloody boots
laying by the side of the bed

only a pair of yesterday's underwear
pile of white socks & dirty bluejeans

no drama
in routine

just the silly unrelenting pain of the days
making a buck to share w/an ex-wife & kids

too many hours to stare at a tv blind
my legs throbbing from standing eight hours at a press

maybe write a poem
probably just think about writing a poem

& watch the numbers on the VCR clock
till my eyes clamp skin

one more man
putting in time

for the lack
of any damn thing else

I should've called her from a payphone but I didn't

worst place in the whole goddamn world
is in your living room w/the lights out

thinking of past people
& your inadequacy

I'm there now

thinking of you

true love
yesterday was one ugly son of a bitch
20 years of worms crawling out the nose of the days

I'm so used to the absolute horror
I miss any beauty or stabs of love between my ribs

this morning I watched my wife sip coffee before work
her nightgown folded just so between her legs

nice breasts & a soft face
hot coffee running thru her lips

the woman was content
time was running according to a plan

I sat across the room
thinking of that little Vietnamese girl

the moment a bullet went into her skull
& onto the hands of her dead mother

I sipped my coffee
choking on the bones

expectantly

fugitive
I don't remember any purpose
other than living one more day

my children have never been
an excuse for my life to continue w/o a razor blade

on a hairy throat

I've lied to myself
& slept alone in a humid room

pain/rage/frustration is the paycheck
an empty wallet laying in a pool of blood

in the alley
behind this apartment

& all I know is
you go it alone

in rooms full of people
who feel as goddamn empty as you do

looking for purpose
in a toilet bowl

a bedroom of a 12x60 trailer, 1975 revisited
a quiet evening sitting in this back room
listening to the box & pounding keys w/my teeth

I'm being discussed by her family
in the living room

their daughter/sister/granddaughter
has no bruises from me or bullet holes in her heart

I never hit a woman once
but I did kill one in the war

didn't even know she was female
till her breast fell in my hand

when I checked the body
w/o a head

tonight
my head is under Sony headphones

there are some rather pissed people drinking my coffee
& eating cold cuts in another room

in a little while
the most furious of the bunch will knock on this door

& demand me

I have nothing to say
to their stupid innocence

their daughter
knew better

keys to a cloud
& afterwards
laying next to her in a warm bed

the sheet still wet
you think of others

different days
sharp faces

hear the last words
of relationships shot directly in the ass

& think about dying
but God is dead & living in Phoenix

put your arm under her head
brush sweaty hair from her eyes

listen to the tunes from the clock radio
stare at the ceiling

waiting for your body
to come home

soap in my eyes
I should've taken her teeth out
in one swipe

yes I should have
made it clean & bloody

sitting in my car
the light still green
she snarled

I've heard enough
of your Vietnam

talk of something pleasant
Bill

I said nothing

the date
was over

the high note
What's a man
got to do

to die
around here?

I've been shot twice
throat slit

had needles buried
in my arms

& held a pistol
to my head

a round in the chamber
& a finger that didn't quiver

more scars
than sense

more lives
than a cat

no lives
at all

the summer of '69
glass of orange juice w/2 shots of vodka
sitting on the porch hidden by awnings

my mother turned to me
& said

I know you're scared
but you'll always have a home to come home to

I sucked in a cigarette flicked the ash into the grill

& said
If I live…

everybody is coming home
dead, Mom

I left for Vietnam
the next morning

hungover
carrying a carton of Winstons on the plane

my mother stayed
& died some

it was my last summer

one for Blacky
son
take that candle out of my eyes

put it out in the sink
next to my razor blades

I'm sorry
but the war is still lit in my mind

it tainted you
it ruined your mother

I can't imagine life w/o it

I am only surprised to be alive
40 is a stupid age for a wild-eyed man

the Amerasian babies we left are adults now
I'm still nineteen years old

walking swamps
looking for their mothers

I have everything
to say

but

sorry

just the players, just the show
you are the war
the blood & the bullet

a puddle of mud
the soft gauze holding your wounded guts

laying in graves w/dead children
standing on your face

bury Mom
bury Dad

your wife is that clump of corpse
cut wickedly up the middle & pitched into a puddle of
rain

the man responsible
fought the war

wrote the poem

pull out my teeth, mama, I'm coming home
don't ask me for forgiveness
I'm not Jesus

I don't care if you come to my funeral
I won't see you/won't know your face

been a week now
crawling quiet in my skin

clutched in the heart of Post Traumatic Stress Syndrome

I can barely talk
when I want to hit your lips w/a fist

smack the smugness
right off a tooth

I am angry tonight
furious & mean

those Purple hearts
aren't invisible

& not
forgiven

pulling a piece out of myself & calling it a watch
I never bothered to take a good hard look at myself
the mirror is every morning & it lies like a rabid dog

give me a seat in a dark room & a little music
I'll tell stories to myself for hours

change the faces
forget the facts

time is not the enemy
I am

the thread holding this skin together is rotted
w/guilt/shame/inadequacy

but it's going to be awhile
before the packing falls out

on the inside
unbroken
& bent

I'm the last teenager alive
the others are walking the paddies of Hell

Joey Buhler never left Con Thien
the flag around his coffin weighed more than the body

Eddie Firestone died in his sleep w/his National Guard unit
his throat slit in 2 by a sapper

Russ Ritenour walked out of Vietnam
& died in a Baltimore room w/a horse in his arm

Eddie Schomer…
Agent Orange killed him before he turned 30

& me
the one no one figured

I wait every day
to die

the lock is frozen & the key is bent anyways
I'll disappoint you
leave the taste of horror in your mouth

the bed is unmade & smells of fear yellowed w/sweat
I forgot the rent, forgot the car payment

the lights are low
I trust nothing but the blackness of a dead living room

there are guns here but no one finds them

food is in the cupboards
bad milk in the refrigerator
a pint of blood on the floor & hair on my comb

don't bother to look for the dust of another woman
she was never here

& yes those are scars

from a knife & a gun

...war not women
the pictures taped to the wall are my kids & dead friends

w/o them
I'd be you

smiling

an individual retirement account
I didn't even make the papers
because I only killed myself

no one lied
they just didn't remember

I had felt like a ghost
a blind phantom
invisible except for a beard

the days felt like a stupid temporary job

& I quit w/o notice

advice
no truth
live the consequences

the end will come quick enough w/pain

look at yourself & crack some teeth
stare at the mirror till you become invisible

no magic to life
just walk right on through

there will always be a cross waiting for your body
ignore it but dream of your death

I've learned more sitting alone in a small room
facing a dark wall & myself
than anything I ever read

sip your pain & regret w/music
& don't remember

sucking my own blood quietly

a not-so-beautiful fool limping from his last accident,
his balls stuck to his heart

the Hell we know is better than a paid-for room in Heaven
…& so easy when there's someone to blame

too late tonight

I'll lay down on this bed in my clothes
prop my head on a pillow & watch the window
not answer the phone or the door
think of ten solid reasons to die but not one good excuse to live

& I'll lie to myself
wonder who I would've become w/o Vietnam
because I already know that asshole

rope trick

3 years into a marriage

I sucked the bones of a few strange women who knew me
& still didn't flinch at my body

slept in my car when I dreamed of sleeping
so busy losing myself in other people

I found nothing…

& I looked right in their faces
I didn't say I was a veteran
because it was like finding a turd in my bed

I talked of drugs
women
music

but not me
my skin's history

there are no gentle words to describe
killing

I don't miss you
I confess all
that's all
I killed men
cheated on my first wife

didn't change enough babies' diapers
& I forget their grownup birthdays some years

I eat bacon & I don't give a damn about cholesterol
death is in my shoes wanting my whole leg

I'm chewing on my beard right now
wanting a cigarette badly

& a touch of innocence
to get me through to the grave

you got a light
buddy?

1976
drugs kept me from killing you
it was less painful to kill myself

I walked the streets of Denver & Chicago
blind crazy w/the taste of war on my hands

my family was a good audience to a county jail cell
a wife wandered back to her incestuous father
my children sat in the back seat for the whole ride

I kept a gut full of reds
sleeping in my shoes

true, absolutely true
life & love
stick a foot in the groove

& it disappears
into a funeral home full of your body

your woman will look in your eyes
seeing the reflection of only herself
you were dead a long time

buddy,

let that blood bag drop
in the arms of a waiting baby

the neighbor flushes her toilet
I know… that black dead feeling of dying

& no one finds your body for days
 a lifeless hand hangs over a dirty bed sheet

not even a dog mourns
the clock ticks on

wake up
start again

like bats flying straight out of hell
I know your pain
the room you're sitting in so quietly

sick memories
of yourself

a future
of a thousand yesterdays

the tv
always on

let the bedroom drawer
be the fingers on your hidden pistol

pills sleep
in their own bottle

wrap the afghan
tight around your legs

trap the very air
& have another sip

cry some
in rage

blame the acid
eating the face right out of your life

despair has given you
20/20 vision

don't go blind
on me

war
the sound comes
an explosion among the wet kissing

the grind of bones
a thump of bodies
flesh stuck together seared

& I'll listen, shake w/breathing & sobs

close my eyes
cover my soul

mountains of sperm fall on me
& the urine washes me away

wish upon a dying star
wash me away
the gutter isn't full yet

tonight I feel like a sweeper bag full of bluebottle flies

dead
spawned out

come here
I want to hold your face

till enough people wail at me from the grave

baby

rock my cradle w/your fingernail
till the blood runs down the bag

I might even forgive myself
for an hour

an honest poem
I've destroyed myself enough
so many years chewing on a lead bullet

poisoning myself w/myself

I don't want to die
but I don't want to feel any better

my ass cheeks have dented a coffin
comfortably half-dead

the night of the gargoyle
the face of a stranger stares out from my face
babies squirm at my touch
I shit blood & snakes

ghosts appear only for me to kill them

give me cold blood
cold rain

silence crossed by flies
& a world drowned
by degrees

I am prepared
there are bits of eternity in my intestines

riding slack
my eyes never leave the body
I slid a round in the chamber like grease

watched the man
& his habits

sweated with him
brushed hair out of his eyes
my legs shook in fear too

I took a big gulp as he was looking to my right
& waxed his ass

wait… it's 1992
I spent the day running forms on a printing press
8 hours of ink & noise

clutching a bullet
to my chest like a blanket
made in Saigon

yeah… these are
the stupid years

hearts, whole handfuls of hearts
it was so much easier when I was younger
those freshly wrapped red scars thrilled

shrapnel is impressive on a twenty year old body
but on a middle-aged horse it feels like arthritis

dead nerves
& just plain pain

not even a wife got pity
for a man who outlives
his scars

living, just plain living
if I don't answer to my name
it might be the devil asking
to stop the awful pounding in my heart

people talking about who they're going to be
as if they weren't living yet

it isn't sadness
but horror
that keeps us from disappearing

we all feel so much pain till we forget
then the pain becomes our mother

all we have to do
keep our promises keep clean
& keep going

it's so damn pleasant
a few hours alone with no telephone

not a knock on the door
the cable not paid for & the tv unplugged

noisy slurp of coffee
long stare out the window

slam in a cassette
make it a sad slow tune

load the .38 with love
hold it in your lap

no one is worth sharing this with
enjoy

song
I am nobody
always nobody
not a father or a brother
not anyone's son

my picture was thrown away in a worn out orphan's wallet
look for me in a basement
alive at night
hearing things that are inaudible

plucking eyes like flowers

another body
old faces move their lips if you give them a minute of life
nobody dies in your mind till your heart explodes
then everybody drops
miles of skin evaporate
you'll stand there limply, weakly
decomposed
the future doesn't begin yet
the prison doors are wide open
they'll come to you sleep in you
hung with punishment

two-headed dog
2 bodies on top of me
still smelling of sweat & life

dripping blood & bowel on my face,
on my stomach, on my legs

I felt the bodies take the shrapnel of our own artillery rounds
2 sacks of filthy death saved my breath later
to be a bad husband & a long-distance father

April 9th, 1970 was a good day

to die

the flag of bleeding meat
I am sick of being a man

death is in my bones
barking where there are no dogs

I am dried up
waterproof

the lonesome odor of oil
the flag of bleeding meat

garrotes me
hands my head back to me

every bone in me
belongs to others

& maybe
I robbed them

shadow to shadow

PTSD
like a bed rocked with the rhythm of a thousand couples

I'm still on crabbed feet
peoples' names carved on my neck with passion

killed more than lived

when I say I saw napalm this morning
I mean I saw napalm this morning
bodies cooked to chicken wings
fish burned in water

fuck 22 years ago
turn your child's eye to this morning: 6/6/92

& when I puked in my car
from the gas & blood fumes

not even a wife had the courage
to kiss my lips

my only love poem
sometime under eight layers of dust
death's wet footsteps
& piss-drenched streets
I'll be waiting for you
leaning in the shadows
with a phantom smile
& eyes full of bleeding fireflies

...a lone cemetery a heart pounding open a tunnel
I'll be there wrapped in garbage

sweet as sin

nothing gleams under a three canopy jungle
everybody got one
a sick vampire stuck on their closet door

it might be their mother or children
a father or a damn orphan with a lopsided grin

always somebody
hung blind with your clothes on their back

they know every single mistake you've made
a whole parade of failure & absolute shortcomings of a man

your own treachery will be markedly pointed out
in a trail of mucous slime that stops at your feet

& you can suck your own blood

right
& hard

counting my winnings at 11:30
so disgusted, my shadow died
exiled to burning water

I've gotten worse with age
my worms are snakes

I live suddenly
touch a face, murder me

every hour is a different acid
the moon splattered with my blood & my children

my suicide was committed at birth
an umbilical cord slit by a black-toothed Cong

crying like the ghost of a dead hummingbird
pecked in the eyes by a lice-ridden vulture

I call him
Dad

alligator city
asleep on a bed of mutilation
this body jerks in electro-shock memories

the sheet is a hanging post
standing in a paddy of rice

a field of liquid human shit
bloated fish nibble at red facial cheeks

the dead poke these orifices with their bones
& the twigs of children

& a sick old lady with Cloroxed teeth & brown nicotine fingers
looked at me for the longest time & asked

remember me honey?

dreams come true
I have tried, kept my fists to my sides
kept my guns out of faces
kept my fire to my stomach
I did better in war

PTSD #2
homicide in the apartment tonight

my wife sitting in the kitchen alone
sobbing without tears, full-body crying

one light is on in the living room
the rest of the rooms are black

I must do something to women
that makes them die,
inside & brutal
even my children don't cry anymore

that's a history

Freight Trains

He was the stupidest son of a bitch I ever worked with, no
common sense & no ability. Printing press rollers were
dumped on the floor; ink slopped into the presses; finger-
prints smeared on paper; & he yawned. 35 years old &
not knowing the difference between grease & oil.

    But. He made it to work early every day in an ancient
Ford four door. I watched him sneak pills out of his
pocket to a mouth missing a few teeth – I never asked. An
idiot, not necessarily harmless. Any man that can smoke
three packs of Kools a day – & not cough up blood – is a
hard hombre smacking of the institution. I gave him
room.

Hogan's Heroes; Gomer Pyle, USMC; Green Acres; My
Mother The Car; The Beverly Hillbillies; Gilligan's
Island; The Brady Bunch; Lost In Space . . . he knew
every actor, every episode. Who was still alive, who died
& when.

O God.

licking lips
I've failed

the world will still turn on my death day
A billion people will not get on their knees
& scream my name
babies will never be named after me

my blood will be burned
in a hospital's incinerator

this keyboard
pitched right into the flames

not about Vietnam but really
I'm sleeping next to a person I despise
my leg thrown over hers
would vomit if it could

I drove alone all night to climb naked into this bed
my car is outside the full-length mirror

this person is dead

the needle in the back of my left eye
When I feel like I'm winning
I scream real loud at the dead babies

guilt. . . pull back the skin on my chest
it'll bleed shame

a pair of grease-stained hands will punch through my heart

& shake yours

#17
a hung head tonight
resting my face on broken body parts

memories of people
I should've killed

or loved

I have a pile of bones ready for the smoking
& a healthy pot of rice

a green face & a first person homicide

so much said…
is that blood

on my windshield?

fightertown
everyone I know is just as fucking whacked as me

I have Vietnam for an excuse
it's kept me from eating a lot of nights

they have bad marriages & lousy jobs
children that hate them & parents that forget them

paying back grant money for a college education
that trained them to clean McDonald's bathrooms

dreams turned to toilets full of human fragility

I got most of my scars in firefights
the dying cut my face in half

the dead keep me up at night
hating me for being alive

how about you?

missed opportunity
the flame gets me the flame gets them

I rolled over on the mattress
my hand fell through a hole my cigarette was burning

next time
I win

I am mean son of a bitch
not one swinging dick writer has ever had the guts
to put down the utter disappointment of his own damn children

he'll sweet talk you about screwing their mother on a clean bed
piss & bitch about changing crappy diapers
& food-drenched clothes

but

it's as if those children vanish after age twelve
his pen runs dry when the pubic hair sprouts

I have a room full of ink & paper, a life of disappointment

fuck 'em

a face dripping with wax
tomorrow I turn 41 years old
41 years of being an alcoholic

thanks
Mom

you're dead

I'm thinking of your tears meeting me at the airport
when I got back from Vietnam in 1970
in a bodybag with shoes

you died alone sweetheart

in the spirit
I'm shaking like everybody else
1,OOO,OOO beds were drenched last night
with desperation & fire

I've only met two people in my life
who had a normal childhood
everybody else looks at their parents through the crosshairs

we all need some one to blame at night
when there's only one body under the sheets

I've walked the apartment floor into an emergency room corridor
wanting to physically wrap my hands around my family's throat

& die a little

they're so lucky
I'm dead

a small note, written on a dollar bill
I'm not sorry there are too many dead people crying in my brain

my mother spent 63 years hiding her death
my father's expiration date was his birth

I found my fear in a triple-canopied jungle
more scared of a wheelchair or a VA bed than an aluminum coffin

suicide was never an option but a way of life

whatever you want to
I am free to hang myself
if my neck is in order

I've fought death like a baby fights birthing

one push
& my head

is on the other side

Christ knew better than ask us for a hand
you want a fucking miracle?
the crisp fact that more people don't commit suicide

is the proof on a knife's edge

the days are relentless
nights crapped out of insomnia

everyone works a bad job
a bad marriage

children hate us
parents hate us

I've been shot a couple times
knifed once in the throat

none of it felt as empty as a five day work week
that wasn't getting any better

in the fields of fire
I remember walking next to him
our hands carrying skulls of newly dead

I've tried to forget
flies collected in my hair

I'm scared you'll stay

that door over there is a portal to hell
sometime when I'm not alive
look for me here on a foggy night
I'll be having a smoke on a familiar blood-stained rock
with some old friends & no sounds

no voices
no mouths

just the movement of wild hearts
becoming stone

bury me
I've been awake ten minutes
& already pissed at yesterday
my rifle has an eye at 5:00 a.m.

the mornings bite a little harder
when we become our mother & father

a dark night fell
& bled to death
on my human sleep

it has been difficult to teach
my bones to disappear

Goddamn
the mystery was gnawed right out of this life
every day smells stale and flat as canned beans

I've looked for years for an answer
a brilliant guide to my time & lungs
& there isn't one

the writers are guessing

the priests lie
purchasing piety & burning our blood

our hopes remain a skeleton

a god was made by man to conceal our cowardice
& the whole earth reeks of heavenly merchandise

there's no forgetting
the tainted years
the blood of men foaming in water

that war slid down greased skids
leaving us dead

killed with the killers
shame's burned fingers are stuck to our faces

my presence is revenge
walking in 12 DD boots

a mad dog in my heart
& a lung full of ash

**they killed the French, the Americans,
then themselves**
the rice bloomed into blood

waking up suddenly with powder burns on my face

I put the blanket over my head
& reloaded

a fair amount
of skin was involved

the October moon melted the Mekong Delta
when you pull my knife out of the wall
there will be a man attached by the palm of his hand

take the knife, forget the man
it's my world drowning in spit

the truth running down my chin
I'll be there
arms wide open
when the worms cry out your name

Vietnam… I needed you
when the parental alcoholism wasn't enough
war has been the best excuse for flushing a man
willingly down a toilet

but really I would have gone down headfirst
without it

I had to pull the car over & swallow smoke
like finding a personal Jesus
every goddamn day I move my body from the bed to the sink

the green hands of the Vietnamese woman I let die
squeeze my brain
honestly she was dead before I opened the door

I don't even believe that

I sat on the mud floor & watched her take a last breath
& did nothing to save her

she hated me
I didn't think of her as human

& now
I can't even crap

without her watching

Saigon
baby you could at least kill me
when you talk love I hear the special silence
of a dead mouth
the flapping of filthy wings

the bluest moon
pale
& quite mad

I am not your father

I'll close & lock the windows
when you turn the gas on full

our souls will spin like dimes on fiery floors

fear nothing
fear me

perfect, absolutely perfect
a night without a telephone attached to it
my heart beating at 50 squeezes a minute

one woman who could smile at my face
a child that loved me without reservation

dead people staying buried, living that remain forgotten

the bathroom toilet flushing without jiggling the handle
a sink that doesn't drip like a knife wound

one window that really doesn't want me to fall out of it
a midnight too dark for an apology

standing here in my birthday suit
you can actually feel death flying around your face in & out
the hole calling your name & wanting your skin

I've shot it
fed it barbiturates

it fucked my mother
& the whole family watched

my birth

when the vet center failed
sleep with
spend every day with

a human being you absolutely despise

yourself

I've lost your Purple Heart

human too
how many more nights alone
I know how I feel
dead

my bed is too full
the worms squirm

with & without you

sweet

lips

1993

look you right in the eyes
dead mother, why do I still dream of you?
I have your skin & unfortunately, some of your thoughts
the neighbors will have called the cops
complaining about the smell from my apartment
I'll be tucked into this chair
animals licking my arms
dead dreaming

put this on my headstone
I've given up on the dead, forgotten most of them by name
but their faces are fingerprints on my wrists
so be it

a freight train making its own tracks
vultures waiting on my flesh, the lies didn't take my soul
but made it not worth fighting for
war desensitized me, I walked over thresholds
not mortal despair but immortal despair
doors have clicked behind me

rips like flesh
when every other vet I know drops Vietnam out of his gums
like it was a hometown
or a damn good mother with a meal on the table

they've lived too long without the hard fear of a dead body
any man can be a hero if he has a paid up beer on the counter

our mythology is impossible
desperate in its valor

you want the truth?
ask our ex-wives

chainsaw evening
when she holds my face in her small bird-like hands
I can feel my death packing a cheap suitcase

here I am
kill me

99% Vietnam
blame your mother, blame your father
blame high school, blame a priest
blame your wife, blame your children
blame the job, blame the bank
blame luck, blame love

but tonight in your sweaty pillow, blame you

straight up
I can't even look at my life without a revolver
people are safer in wallet-sized pictures
lots of pointed fingers within a foot of my face
righteously give me your guilt & a drop of your blood

I'll sleep like a child

A straight shot
everybody wanting a reason to live,
everybody needing a reason to die
I wonder what my kids think
honestly having a father so wound into the grave
their heads under the covers studying pain
some places you just can't go
even if you run till your heart comes out of your throat

if anyone had said in the Nam
that I'd be sitting in a cold December room when I was 41
writing & staring out the window
at a dead dog piled on the garbage can
I'd have rolled their words & smoked them
my future has never been thought

I fell into kids & a marriage
my job was a newspaper want ad & a previously unhappy man

not much thought hung on the spokes of Bill Shields
running the days on full guts & a small asshole drifting

I kept what you gave away

98 %
my mother was my worst excuse, my father was the next

I learned nothing from their lives
like listening to the telephone ring over & over
without answering

they bloodied themselves over time & spousal hate
I have too

& when it occurred to me that I was finally alone
I didn't leave the couch for a month

then
I burned it

scraping the ceiling with my neck
everything tries to kill us
every damn thing we crave has the juice running down the coffin

you don't have to leave the house to die

I survived needles & a marriage
but not the memory, which is better

gimme pizza & a rope

I want a clean-shaven shine laying in a purple box held by tongs

I'll like it

terror
it's not poetry
the sound of sobbing cracks the heart
teeth chattering from the cold
TB blood
a can for piss, a can for shit
a death half-gone
pain, hunger, human worms, a jail cell
it's better than that

horror's long, long night
lie still
let the flowers scream
whisper blood on a face

if you hear your breath, you're only half-dead

eat your soul for supper

Hell doesn't want a full stomach
but it can't wait for your bare feet

crunching bones

some dogs are meant to be put to sleep
when my wife's face starts to melt into the image
of the little girl I killed purposefully in war

a spine lurches forward suddenly
when the phone rings

night sweats
crawling through dreams on the blades of bloody knives

& when I talk to you
I might as well be buying groceries off the shelf

fuck it
Honey

save me a seat in
that big black

Fleetwood
hearse

bone dry
10:45 p.m.
I reminded my eye to blink & water slightly

if I had a soul it would be buried in the garbage can
under the hair of my unborn children

the tv hums like a cheap light bulb in an old man's lamp

after all the war & death I saw as a stupid kid
I should have known the life would essentially be insipid

a sip of cold coffee
stare at the eyes on the wall

tomorrow is already
here

self-hate
I blow cigarette smoke at the picture of me on the wall
put my middle finger right between the eyes of that
photograph

the flies
wave back

a lame poem that needs leg braces, a heart/lung machine
a fish slapping on my tongue
I killed the light an hour ago
got coffee, got cigarettes, got tv in my veins

a man can step on heads
4:47 a.m. on any given Saturday morning

one ass
one chair

king of the sewer

five dollars, five times
the bruises on my leg aren't getting any better
follow my wife's finger to the alley, my next hotel room
there's no bomb in my heart but one in my head
the fuse wound through my teeth

one more day

that's all

vampires singing in the rain
when no one's coming to save you
and you finally accept that hope is in a landfill
and your family shows you their backside
and the landlord's spit is all over your wallet
and your kids don't recognize that voice on the phone
and you turn the radio up in the car
just so you won't hear the engine bleed on the street
and know that home is where everyone else lives
and you never connected the phone
and you always pick up the mail
and that's the sound of your sick heart pounding
against bony ribs so loud it echoes the blood in your ears
and you hate those fucking tears running down your nose
and what you touch feels so pitiful desperate
because it is

an ounce of skin, or less
the men slipping through the palms, dressed in black and blood
is my image, the damn theme of my smoked lungs, diseased
heart
everything – my job, wife, kids, and goddamn me – is a situation

this is my letter

I don't expect a reply

I don't care about you
those years of hiding Vietnam behind my bloody teeth
employers never knew till the inevitable call from the VA man
explaining my behavior, the time spent in the violent ward
my ex-wife still won't discuss those years I wrote her letters
a couple kids were diapered in my disability money
…all those years of self-destruction and silence
weren't cured by a 12 step program or another religion
they weren't cured

walking the haunted field
I'm easy to find but not in a phonebook
hell, I'll meet you halfway if you're a vampire
write a decent poem and I'll put away my .41 magnum
when you knock on this apartment door

anonymous, without applause,
I'm close enough to tie your shoes

those with facial scars already have my address

I like it better in a small room
a chair silhouetted in my sweat
the wall with my blood stain that turned into black caulking
I locked the door an hour ago, turned on the stereo
and been thinking about dead women I've known
women at least dead to me, and it feels about right
I'm alone, like I know I should've been
one body in the bed, ten solo fingers

if it moves
kill it

surfing Saigon
mother's son
dying

an acre of corpses
thousands of blue flies
swim in the eye juice of the dead

it wasn't Gettysburg
but me, sitting in a room in Pennsylvania,

watching blood run down the walls of another apartment
...somewhere in there my bones might be found

wrapped in shaved words

flood
fearing nothing
but myself & another quiet evening

I need a starless night
a pair of blind eyes staring at me from the bed

some men will do any damn thing to stop the trembling miserable
with their feet stuck in concrete boots, heads in the coat hanger

I'm one of those

a dull moment
a fresh hole in a sky-blue ceiling
& the landlord wants the man's name who fired the round

he's my age, got the bad bad guilts over not doing
a life sentence in Vietnam

& in my own pitiful way
I'm sending him there

monthly

that died too
tuck the ghosts behind my back
some of them killed, the rest forgotten or buried
I can't even make love to a woman without seeing faces
my sweat is the blood running
down the crack of a dead person's ass

stripping away my life with memories

bubbling up bone

& skin

fuck it, Homer, I gave what I had
my capacity for death overwhelms everyone but me
the fact is: we die, with & without flowers or love

bodies buried, bodies flamed, it doesn't matter
rip away the romanticism
forget the phone call

me too
shivering at the bland face of nothing

rock

roll

This was never written on a Dollar bill
forget love
forget the hate

every day is milk gravy
walk 24 hours bleeding from every hole

the pain, the unforgiven loneliness are the chrome in our eyes
we have the time & the fear to eat supper

no one's coming
to save you
or me

amen

Too many nights, too few days
so lonely that the room spins
as the head is hidden under a pillow

a hand holding the floor
& sweat beading on the feet

I bought a ticket for the whole show
the whole bleeding bag of man

1 bed
1 body

it always
makes sense

A.M. Friends

I know your problems & they're no different than mine
no money, an ex-wife's deathgrip on a skinny wallet
too many cigarettes bought from convenience stores
cars that milk the mechanic's crotch
disappearing women, forgotten children,
phones that ring at 3:00 a.m.
that continual nightmare you can't remember in the morning,
(& the one you live through all day)

by god
I just want some pancakes this morning
served by a robot with a face like a wolf

Hung by the throat till the asshole shakes a bit

reassure
& condemn

the afterlife is a grave.
I want the world to die with me

nothing
no one

will change
enough

for
dirt

some nights I sleep in god's goddamn cradle
nobody called
nobody is coming

another lifetime
before I get home

stiletto shoes
left in a dirty corner

some men lit their bedrooms on fire as kids
& the firemen didn't pull the bodies out

connoisseurs of cigarettes & abused women
every day the final call of the razor blade

the green teeth in the mirror belong to a face

the dreams, the lies & all that green air
4 pair of socks
6 shirts
4 pants
1 pair of shoes
cassette player
cd player
4 inches of canceled checks
assorted bathroom paraphernalia

a box of music
carton of books
the dying truck
a man coughing up his lung

there it is…
what I own

what I
should

Chocolate Town
days of night
if there was ever any talent, I sold it at the flea market

I looked at the map
till I became the city

suffering is not a can of Spam
dying is not a spare toothbrush left by the sink

living is not this Sunday morning
12/12/93

balls, two handfuls
I can't remember one
that didn't shake her head
& say

you're one sick motherfucker

These same women sat for hours listening to my Vietnam
horror stories after I woke up screaming, clutching
hands & throats.

they had compassion, guilt & fear
& they stayed a long time, which can be a night or a life.

But they would leave,
the smell of finality covering the carpet like a grave.

There's so much blood to clean up
living alone, dying alone

I don't need
band-aids

Kicked in the ass by the blue veins of life
I got the time & the soul to piss away
if I drop tomorrow, there'll be no surprise birthday party.

Expendable as soiled underwear
& as predictable.

There was a time I thought about catching an AK-47 bullet
in my mouth and it felt right.

Dying is nothing at nineteen
though a nineteen year old won't agree

I'm going to light another cigarette,
chew on some fatty red meat & sip a little coffee.

The disappointment
cringes in my corner.

1994

the day I catch my soul falling through a throat
nothing left
never was

I shouldn't have kicked Christ in the balls
stopped drinking & thrown my syringe into another's vein

Vietnam is shit 24 years after the fact
it's been my worst excuse for being no damn good

no damn good at all

I've lied to myself staying alive
promised the kids I'd breathe till they turned 18

& now they are
& I can stop huffing

but won't

& these are no reasons at all

except for the known emptiness
of a man's disguise

I really fucking hate you
a forest fire for a brain
blood bursting in one eye, ears charred to lumps

I have sat on couches & been destroyed
slept in beds that ate my face

& crapped my vanishing personality

there's so much self-inflicted violence
holding a chin in ten mutilated fingers

as if beauty
was never a beast

I hope to Christ
that you too aren't pounding the floor tonight with cramped
feet
          & a whipped mind
that someone answered the call & remembered the voice
that the car has gas, the wallet a twenty dollar bill
that all those screams are your neighbors
that your week has more than forty hours in it
that the registered mail was a mistake
that the furnace stays on, a toilet flushes
there's a can of soup for the morning
that the person underneath the covers is better than all of us
& that tomorrow ain't today

blowing through the cracked lips of loneliness
tonight, if there was a heaven
I'd stomp you through the ground till your head touched a sky

your pain, sweetheart, can't save your ass
or make another one disappear

dying is living
without air

the nursing home & the gravestone are a shuffle away
bathrooms in both, chrome rails to hold your hands

angels dressed
in orthopedic shoes

dead you
dead me

the steel canopy
my ears wear suicide
like a missing wallet full of twenties

I wouldn't recognize my dead mother
if she sprang from the grave & gave me a kiss

my dead daughter has turned her face away

an ex-drunk, an ex-addict
a permanent stupid Vietnam veteran

there is no one to call at 2:12 a.m.
when the phone line has been gnawed by the dead

but if I could
would you answer?

I wouldn't

ex-wives, children,
the sound of bare feet on a linoleum floor
two could kill me
one will

so many guns to place on my face
it'll only take one bullet

& a good eye

by your own hand
that sickness hanging like dead cats from coat hangers
I understand checking my blood at the door

there's murdering secrets crawling down my legs
the Viet Cong are sleeping at the foot of your bed

this shaking
isn't malaria

DIE MOTHERFUCKER:
AN OPERA

beneath the words was a blooded pack of lies
A hard trigger pull for an angry man…

He stood at the foot of the bed & his wife slept at the end
of the gun. The Sunoco sign across the street pinned his
shadow against the wall, with others who drop no shadow.

Focus goddamnit,

squeeze

Young women & baby Vietnamese jumped his eyes, tore
the hair right out of his heart. Humiliated, the man stuck
the magnum back in his underwear drawer & laid back
down beside the woman he so wanted to bloody.

She didn't stir.

He weighs nothing.

Ask him.

poppers
The screwdriver slipped & his left eye caught it.

He wasn't standing next to him nor was he even in the same town.
Frankly, he didn't give one fuck about this man.

He lost that eye.

home forever

Flies swarm his head, sit on his eye lids & walk the bridge of his nose. Absently, he swatted them away but never blinked.

He had that stare, the eyes to look at a man's hands from two hundred meters & know them.

Dead man eyes.

Pools of misery in a VA bed.

as wicked as it seems

His mother took absolute care of him; made the bed, fed him at 6, packed a school lunch everyday, solved the inevitable problems of being a kid & later a teenager.

They slept in the same room till he was fifteen.

When he killed his first man in Vietnam, his mother pulled the trigger.

He did the next one by himself.

a night pounding the ears into pancakes

As she stood there, her pale blue nightgown blending into the wall & a smile falling out her eyes, I never saw the knife.

Right here, on the corner of my face.

A baby cried, a dog barked for his full bladder. The light in our kitchen was still out.

Cold.

psycho killer

He sits in his car in the middle of the night, playing with the radio's knobs, shifting his feet around the gas & brake pedals; the body is slumped down low in the seat, eyes even with the dash, watching people go in & out of the apartment building.

This man falls asleep with the motor running, waking up with a carbon monoxide headache & a dry throat.

The blades of a downed helicopter rip him to shreds.

you want reality, motherfucker

His time was up. The vile dreams of Vietnam were gone, as were the grey body parts that he would see in his peripheral vision. Even the anger left his acidic stomach.

One call to his kids, another to a damn good woman.

He spent an hour lugging books out to the garbage cans & another ripping cassette tapes apart. His clothes were in paper bags on the kitchen floor.

There was nothing left in his bowels to give anyone.

He sat on an old green couch & waited thirty-one days to die.

& he did die.

heart attack

It was a diabetic syringe he found in the garbage can at work. He locked the bathroom door & stuck it in his arm. Pulled back a little blood.

He closed his eyes. A corpsman screamed, "We got wounded here!"

A snake wrapped around his arm & kissed him on the cheek.

the Tet Offensive

He only wanted to rent a woman's sexual organ for an hour & two squeezes of his prostate gland. He had long ago lost the questionable ability to small talk a bar stool & the ass attached – so much easier when the bucks are stuffed into the mouth without a word.

She was maybe 21 & maybe not; it doesn't matter.

& he fucked her without passion, a machine needing a shot of oil. She didn't say a word about his scars & he smacked an extra twenty into her hand.

Feeling good

was good enough.

widowmaker

He has always liked to watch people sleep; kneeling next to their bed, he'll lightly touch their face with his finger-tips & laugh very quietly.

His daughters will never remember him by their beds – he was so unobtrusive after the war – as he spent hours combing hair out of faces & whispering,

"Daddy's home"

All night long.

burning the Phoenix down

Carrying 3 heads in his right hand, he slumped against the thatch wall & lit a cigarette. It was a burned ville, the jungle hung against its side.

He had two hours to kill. 3 heads to talk to & a cramp to work out of his hand. The cigarette was snuffed out on the man's head. He slept briefly, fingers wound around the hair of a man, another man & a woman.

Then he cut their faces off.

grease fire in the baby's crib

A loneliness there is no name for.

The despair of a lost bullet.

He hides himself in women & children, jobs & a set of headphones; always a smile of recognition in a stranger. No close friends but a steady chair weekly at the local AA meeting. There is a Purple Heart stuck in the corner of his wallet, next to the picture of his dead daughter – but no one knows this. No one.

Catch this man's eyes unaware & you'll see the graveyard opened & the bodies burning in the sun.

He just might see you.

reminiscing on a sharp pain between the heart & bowel

This young man looked up from the e-z chair, an eye bloated in blood & a homemade bandage around a wrist.

A kerosene heater on the floor stunk worse than his two packs of cigarette smoke; his two kids were watching tv in dirty grey diapers & sucking Koolaid out of baby bottles.

"What the hell?" he asked his brother.
"I married her, motherfucker." he answered.

for a deaf corpse waving its arms wildly
You can tell him anything, put your head down & whisper your failures, the men & women that sold your trust to dogs, the cancer that's eating your bones into cereal, your failed child, the bottle underneath the car seat, a scab you can't leave alone, the woman or man you masturbate to, the dream that never will come true.

& like you, he's so consumed by his own pain, the man chews off his ears.

Quietly.

advice from a man who should have died in Vinh Long
don't panic death
let the idiot next door dance on its floor

there are a thousand lies about Heaven & Hell
& they are lies

no one comes back
no one

the junkie with a needle in his arm
feels just as immortal as you

& he is

your grave is to be expected & despised
I've seen hundreds of deaths

each one wanting another minute, another day
one more chance to kill the guilt

well… it ain't in the bottle

you'll never know when your lips turn blue
your blood riding the sleeves of the embalmer's shirt

stomp hard
pound fists through clocks

this time
is yours

see Blondie — a poem not about death
she gets very drunk before lying down with me
her hand reaches for my body vaguely

I laugh to myself
thinking — if this is what it takes

I'll take it

we've kept in touch since the war
just a card in my post office box
"hey man, you oughta come up here to Montreal

it's killing"

he'll sign it with a dead man's name
as a joke & a signature

slap a bloody fingerprint
over my address

another one calls my answering machine late at night
and whispers,
"don't you ever forget Cau Mau.. ever"

he doesn't have to worry
I can't

Jim Cooper sent me his broken fingernail last year
so I wouldn't

thank
you

white trash
I followed my father's footsteps & left my kids
when they were sitting on the toilet

he did W.W.II
I did the Nam

he got remarried
me too

at 73 he found God
at 41 I find nothing

Dad shuffles his feet
& his wife harps at his alcohol

I've never asked him
if he sees dead German soldiers on his front porch;
maybe time has been good to him

& they faded like last winter's snow banks

He's never asked me if I'm seeing dead Viet Cong
I must be that obvious

hoping he sees the grave
before me

when you hate everything you've done to your life
You've got to be desperate or an idiot to sleep with me
I'll probably grab your throat during the night

a gun is more reassuring
than I am

the night turns blacker
my face flashes in the sky

some men should have died young
buckets of pain poured into their graves

I know one
who should be left alone

to lick his brain

after a lifetime whining about Vietnam:
a 4-word poem
my mistake: one coffin

BACK TO THE WALL

American Hero
The man stepped right up, feet on top of a case of bottled beer. He placed his neck into a rope noose that was strung from the light fixture. He pulled it tight and leaped to the floor.

He hung for less than a minute, thinking nothing but the pain as he spun slowly in a circle; the spots in his eyes were bright red when he took a palmed razor blade and cut the rope, falling chest-first into the kitchen sink.

Then he packed his lunch for work.

Vietnam Veteran #9
No more, he screamed to himself under the shower. Not one more minute of this shit. He turned the water off, toweled his hair, dressed, checked the mirror for a person, then walked into the kitchen and ate a raisin bagel.

Searched his pockets for change to make a phone call.

Forget 'em, he said to the tv and the walls and the roaches. They're dead.

sights along hell's highway
He stood 6'4" and weighed around 240.

He hadn't meant to hit her above her left eye. There were so many reasons not to… but there it was and no one can take back a bruise.

"I never meant to hit you," he said from the other side of the living room. She said nothing when he walked back to the bedroom and packed his clothes.
And left her life.

His wife never heard this story.

an impressionistic mystery story of the Vietnam war
A small rooster ate the white worms as they fell; the child finished, pulled up her black pants and grabbed her mother by the leg.

An old woman spat betel nut juice between her squatted knees.

Two fires. Twelve grass huts. Old crippled people, young mothers, younger kids – a full cemetery.

I know who killed them all.

as spiders stare back in the mirror
He's left pieces of himself hanging from the sky and dangling from the floors of Hell.

A finger severed in a rice paddy marked only by an artillery coordinate; a chunk of his chin dropped into a swamp seven weeks and two miles from his finger; teeth fell in bars from Florida to Colorado; a motorcycle tore an ounce of his skin and fed it to a car; one toe is buried behind his ex-wife's trailer; a hospital in Maine burned a chunk of his guts in their incinerator.

His eye will never blink as he shakes your hand.

Stranger.

D.O.A.
She had a career. He had a job.

Evenings were quiet together. They finished each other's sentences. No kids, but a phone. Housework was ripped up the middle of the apartment.

She was stable, working the same job for years. Paying bills on time and actually had an IRA; her parents visited regularly. His history was too quiet and his family was dead before his eyes.

Three days before every stinking payday she would help him out with gas and a few folding dollars.

It wasn't perfect, but it worked for a lot of years.

The bedroom wall is still dented from the bouncing of tennis balls against the plaster. Her hair is in the cracks.

the truest story
Nobody found him.
He was lost where a man leaves no footprints.

The room had sandbags piled on the windowsill, a wire screen in front of the glass to deflect a grenade. He rolled the sleeping bag up in the morning and placed it on the foot of the bed. There was a loaded gun within an arm's reach from anywhere in that pit.

A broken eight track tape the spiders found...

His mother cashed the VA checks each month and brought him cigarettes, chow, and the tv guide; his picture was framed in the living room.

Before Vietnam.

In love with the grotesque and the self-mutilated

1. An old man's fingers pull a government check out of the box.

2. The coroner had to rip the skin off his wrists to pull off the montagnard bracelets a village chief welded on him in '70.

3. The day Eddie Skomer was born, Aug. 12 1951, his father left for Korea.

4. He had been a boy scout, a football player, pulled a little guitar, had the usual acne and wore high-water pants through highschool.

5. His old man never worked a day after the war.

6. There were faceless brothers and sisters. A mother beaten by life.

7. Eddie left town the day after graduation and joined the Army.

8. Three years later he came home. Halfway whole.

9. His car stayed drunk for a year.

10. A marriage lasted long enough for the skin to turn white under his ring.

11. The kids were adopted by her new husband.

12. The first spot was found in his right lung, the second on the liver. He had five chins from the anti-inflammatory drugs that caused his body to swell.

13. A hearse brought him home from the VA hospital.

14. His kids got the money.

15. I got the bracelets.

my prayer as a Vietnamese gesture of food
We were all just stupid jokes. The jackals that ran amuck
screaming violent nightmares to four bare walls that only
our demons could spot with blood. We died stuck full of
self-agony. Men as cartoons – the slow drip of vomit
running down a filter-tipped Lucky Strike.

But what few of us that are left
can eat your bloody tomb flowers.

Amen.

DEAD POEMS

#1
teeth in a trash bag
still hands that weigh more than a body

the goddamn pain that drove a man wild with fear & shame
ends on a velvet pillow to be burned with his fat

I waited my life for this quiet moment

it's here

#2
the woman next to me patted my leg
I felt my doll eyes blink

there was just a ceiling & a bed
one woman & me

it was the emptiest moment

a grave opened
& I walked out

#3
tears running down my puffy face
is the same as walking on the moon in tennis shoes

it hasn't happened yet

life itself crushed the self-pity out of my face
hospital beds & cruelty are much more understandable

I am
what you see

invisible

#4
a bag of shit with two eyes
a grown-up child walks up, pulls open the sack

& says
I hate you

Dad

#5
after ten years of running printing presses for myriad idiots
I have the same bills & a cheezy wallet loaded with body lint

as if
3650 days have not been enough for one man

they
haven't

#6
when the poets talk of flowers
I want them placed on their banal graves

big bloody hearts
hanging from a copperhead's mouth

a SASE
attached

#7
no the demons are not angels stripping your life from your death

all you got is the person behind your face
period.

the only demons are bad memories
a personal history drawn in purple markers by autistic children

& the angel is hanging its head
crying in a soiled kitchen towel

they've all
left you

alone

#8 — tribute to Richard Brautigan
in those thirty days before they found your body
the squirrels ate good, flies too

you silly bastard
suicide...

it's too late
to come back

Dick

#9
permanent fireflies
in my eyes

an entire life
not waking up in the morning

smacking my head on the pillow every night
depending on an ambulance without lights to pick me up

a little blood in my bowels
dizzy with a cigarette

I promised myself not to use the vile word Vietnam
in these poems of the dead & living mutilated

but there is nothing else on the shelf to grab

I have no future
past this bedtime

#10
cannon fodder for the undertaker
our tragedy is not on any map or restaurant guide

a suit of my skin is ripped with age
I can rub fingers through my brain

expendable as a paper plate

here's a life
God

kill
it

#11
falling down into the arms
of my dead parent's blue veins

my mistakes & failure haven't been original
I followed the bloodline of my white trash ancestry

our children couldn't know us
as we blinded them with razor deceit

a mother that knew the asshole in the mirror
but not the turd underneath

& everyone has a father that doesn't give a damn
yes indeed

we die
the lie

#12
ghosts singing like my phone ripping its plastic guts out
then being handed to me with a voice whipping on the line

the nights
are nights away from home

the damned dead never stay buried till we die with them
our bones buttered on their toast

the living
are worse

they

never shut
the fuck
up

#13
I don't need a river to drown in
or the ceiling of a jail cell to hang from

my throat is pals to a syringe
& a cigarette

everything I need is under my fingers, scarred
it doesn't take a grocery list to suicide & live

I have my own river
my own jail

a rainbow
included

#14
revenge…
that'll be Heaven

I kicked my afterlife right in the fucking head
no prayers, no answers & no more questions

give me a vivid image
an hour to pound a keyboard

a window to stare out of
& a car that starts first time every time

one woman with some dirt under her nails

I don't need Christ
to carry me down the well

#15
the little kids are waiting impatiently for the next Christmas
& the old men whisper in pain, "God, bring me home"

I've built thirty-seven fires in this dirty-windowed room
blew a quart of snot & chewed my fingernails to the nub

there's been a good bit of hatred flung on the carpet
some human, some history with sympathetic muscles

learning
to pace

the graveyard
mind

#16
the cat dropped the dead mole from his fangs on the kitchen
carpet as a birthday present for me

I got a person between the sheets

for him

#17
the sirens sang off-key standing on my bag of skin
nipping my face with the gums of the dead,
swatting my eyes with scaly grey hands

they looked familiar as convenience store clerks
or members of my family, my own children, myself

I gave them nothing but another evening of tv

#18
the day angels drag your head across the floor
I'll hold the garbage can lid in my hand

there is so little to be thankful for
so don't be

you asked no one to be born
you ask everyone to die

there's a nightmare in my pocket
tailor-made for your dog whine

I got a demon
you might like

too

#19
blue faces
starry mouths

more comfortable with memories than realties
alone I sit with hundreds, thousands of interpreters
clutching their hands to a stainless-steel cross as I lip read:
gonna die more

they bore the Hell
right out of me

#20

I'm leaving my rage inside the damn kids
no coffin lid is going to suffocate my life

everything exploded into human rain
the heart, brain, kidneys, bowels screwed forcibly from a
man's body

not every part of me can be washed
from the kitchen floor of the jungle

here's my blood

pitch it

#21

the silent life
in a noisy room

walk the carpet till the spidery veins of a mother disappear
there will always be people you can't kill with a gun

as you stare down a memory akin to meaningful suicide
wrapped in the grey plastic bag of a mind

tied at the end
by a clot of your favorite blood type

#22
a bad taste
in my soul

one more temporary person with the permanent appetite
sniffing a kleenex for a taste of last night
punctured badly by a syringe of a gravedigger's dream

& all I know
is 2 feet, 2 hands

the pictures in an empty wallet

#23 — a love story, of sorts
I want to touch your face in the dark
really brush my fingers against your cheeks

they'll be stars in the coffin
dry blood flaking off our bones

we can fall through each other
as our children's graves spin

there just might be forever
in our very human mud

here

#24
cut me
baby

show me some human qualities tonight with dirty hands
I need you to laugh at my face,
sneer at the scars running the highway down my neck

there's a red thread holding this skin together
clip it

I've already called your parents
to take out this trash

#25
I put your makeup on
fixed your hair nice

kissed you goodbye
before the police & the coroner came

& rolled those old stockings back up to your knees

it was me that stuck the fifth of vodka in your wooden box
that your kids lowered by strings into the dirt

I don't think you slept
too long in Hell

Mom

#26
I've always needed another life to ruin
a wife, a small child, the close friend & all that trust
I pocketed into green lint

my head banged a hole through the bedroom wall
their bodies filled it sloppily

this damn world better die
when I do

#27
all this pain
all this dribbling

I got a bag here with my head in it
it's yours with no blood attached

you can have all the failure & deceit that fell out of those lips-
feel the lies soaking up through your feet

it's a loaded place
without a gun

& a fingerprint

#28
you whispered in my mouth
come home, baby

I lit a cigarette &
said I'm trying

6 rounds
leaped for the chamber

like the mailman
was on his way

#29
living on nothing
dying from everything

scrub my skeleton clean
& leave the drainage

for angels

#30
unrecognizable roadkill
my eyes welded into another man's skull

as if I turned around
while urinating

#31
& when she looks right down
at you & says

how could you?

they never know
how easy it is

dying
before supper

#32
& after all the bodybags have been buried with the memories
of whole human beings picked to skin pieces by the dreams of
a nation

I am still here & that means nothing

it was so much easier having kids

& leaving them

#33
a graveyard tramp
cannibal with the beard & a MAC card

the best memories I've had of this life are grim & obscene
arterial blood is my image, not a soaking Kleenex

killers
kill

our dreams laid out on the concrete pillow like roadmaps
for diseased souls & butchers

a side of beef
as a future

#34
the hair of the hanged man is the most sensitive
I've hidden my pain in a rotten tooth

the next vacancy for God isn't coming from a smoking gun
or a middle-aged man in Youngwood PA on a Thursday night

slurping pizza under the glow
of pale green walls

a wife
on the phone

cigarette smoke blue enough to roll into a dead sky
with bright white eyes

#35 — me too
even after Vietnam & cancer, dead babies swimming in my bones
I'm still scared of living & more scared of dying too late

my body is too full of hate for a demon or a relationship
my eyes too blind for a stair climbing ghost

an asshole wide enough for the cross

LIVING IN HEAVEN – GO-ING TO HELL

the smell on the altar

& all he wanted was some time to think, a couple hours to forget the bad memories that drowned under his eyes.

Two lousy hours of hot coffee & a tv set.

It was a dull paring knife that cut the phone cord, a three inch nail that stuck the door to the frame, an old flowered sheet hanging blind on the window.

Just beautiful, he thought, just me & me

not counting bodies.

one of those beautiful Spring days

Just an old dog, blind & crippled by humans, limping into the street; the white cataracts in her eyes felt the fear of tires but not the direction.

I grabbed her; she was shaking too much to bite. I took her home. My carpet was empty enough for those old bones.

She drank a little milk, then lay beside the bed. After an hour she quit shivering & slept like a tired old lady who's been carrying groceries all damn day.

I put her to sleep the next day.

Don't figure that.

just the sound of the sink dripping
By the time he made it home from work, she was already drunk & on her second pack of generic smokes. Dishes on the sink, crumbs on the rug.

The old leg hurt worse than at work, the vein thumping against his bluish skin; a clot could actually be felt.

In the bathroom he turned on the fluorescent light & dug around in the cabinet for a fresh safety razor. He whispered to himself, you bastard & cut down on that clot.

One of her favorite towels went into the garbage can

with him.

the simple act of making toast
He made himself focus on the chrome side.

His right hand jerked toward the red wires inside & he pulled it back. Focus on the chrome, wait on the bread… simple, don't be greedy with your skin.

At 41, there were so many reasons for this man – but mainly, the glue that holds an hour or a minute together had worn off his daylight tomb.

Feeling dead is impossible for a hungry gut.

prose haiku, a true story
& she said, "I've slept with 217 men.
193 of them are still alive."

living in heaven, going to hell
everything in his life was smooth as a buttered skillet – the wife, the kids, the house, the bills, even the job was a weak breeze.

Then

he knew he must of died in a car wreck months before.

terminal
ask the homeless
or a dog waiting on the gas.

I'll feel more at ease when the horns jut from the heads of
my family; when a snake looks back at me from the
fogged bathroom mirror; it'll be better the day the lizard
scales fall like pennies from my children.

Here's the word: final.

Final men.

a heart thrown on the ground
He watched the small paraphernalia of life – the tooth-
brushes, key rings, laundry baskets, discarded coffee cups,
hair on the carpet, book titles, the hand-drawn signs
hanging at the convenience store & the numbers on his
car's radio dial.

There has to be more than this he thought. I've fallen
into Hell & they've disguised it as Pennsylvania. I re-
member my death... my life. It wasn't this stupid.

He checked himself: pants, shirt, shoes, socks, a wallet
with a paycheck stub stuffed next to a stranger's driver's
license.

He became that man & went shopping.

For hearts.

advice from the bone dice man

an ear for an eye
leave the trace of a man but eat the mangled happy
dreams

if you can save the babies from drowning
carry an organ donor card like a lottery ticket for the dead
doctor

leave the mirrors for the living & the vain
your teeth will eventually be left in an anonymous trash
bin

that much
I know

fucking lame bewildered

one shot no pain
walking soft on the rug, old potato chips cracking under
the toes
a stack of rented books fallen into a couch
rodents stick their heads up behind a leg

the moans of a woman asleep in a vicious nightmare
patting the pillow to not find my head or heart

I'm here
home

MILLIONS OF EYES

Goddamn ghosts.

My daughter was asleep in her crib; the old man lightly brushed the hair out of her face; his six inch chin whiskers stuck between the crib's bars.

The other kids were asleep in another room and he always left them alone. He liked the newborn; the fresh living.

I never had visions; snakes never crawled my skin and bugs left me alone. But I was the only one who ever saw him, this black pajama Viet Cong. A definite dead man.

Our family didn't discuss war; hell, it had been over for a few years, yet the old man and I never stopped chatting.

"She miss a breath, Beel." he said, his hand on her itty-bitty chest.

"Apnea, Chuck. I got the same thing."

"I hate it."

"I don't care."

❖ ❖ ❖

A normal place… the walls painted in an extended Bambi scene and the kids added color to it with crayons. It was awful, all those stick people with fish hands prancing on my eyes.

My wife was going through a phase of waffles, maple in the morning, chicken at night. We fed a lot of dogs.

Our carpet was a patchwork of hundreds of remnants glued to the floor. You'd never find the Kool-Aid stains on it.

I couldn't wait to go to work every day.

⊠ ⊠ ⊠

Chuck came from Hanoi to our duplex in Pittsburgh… His home gone, wife dead, children missing, even his grave was farmed over. He had been in No Man's Land on the DMZ. A B-52 strike literally dissolved his body in '68. He can't remember anything about it – no pain, no heaven. Years of nothing… it felt like life itself.

Then me.

His English poor; my Vietnamese terrible.

He appeared one night after the Carson show as I sipped a cup of coffee alone in the living room. He sat next to me.

"Eh, boy," he said, though actually the first words were unintelligible. "This is?"

"Pittsburgh." I replied, my cigarette burning a hole in the coffee table.

"Which?"

"Pennsylvania."

"I don't understand," he sang back, looking at the crayoned wall. And then folded as quickly as last night's sneeze.

I'm sure he said, "Shit… " on the way out.

⊠ ⊠ ⊠

My wife wore sterling silver fingers, wrists, neck; turquoise pitted in. She had long black hair, baby fine, that clung to her shoulders. This woman came from an upper Midwest family that believed in the Church, Sears, and incest. Her old man smoked straight Camels and her mother spoke through a nasal passage.

I hated them. They hated me.

We circled each other like foamed-mouthed dogs.

My marriage was in trouble before the kids fell like rain. Bobbie and I had sex in common and nothing else and that soon wore to skin boredom.

Contempt breeds familiarity.

❖ ❖ ❖

I come from Nowhere Pennsylvania. A white trashville of trailer parks, donut shops, old women that spend their lives working the counter at Woolworth's, adolescent kids who smoke a pack a day, bars floors they sweep the eyeballs off of, old men with spit running down grey faces… auto part stores, chiropractors, dead teenagers.

One road going in

same going out.

❖ ❖ ❖

When you wake up in the violent Psych ward in the middle of the day, wired to the sockets in Thorazine, there is only one thought:

Fuck it.

❖ ❖ ❖

(a brief interlude of a marriage)

The sight of the ring...

The sight of all the blood.

⊠ ⊠ ⊠

"What the hell?" I asked the old Chuck who was sitting in one of those government chairs by my bed.

He wouldn't answer me.

So.

I asked again.

"MOTHERFUCKER, WHAT AM I DOING HERE?
(then lowercase) And
what the hell is... here ?"

The guy in the next bed was picking at himself, singing real softly like a battery sizzling in the heat.

My hands were strapped to the bed rails – hell, I was spread legged and it didn't feel like Christ dying on the cross.

I screamed

then pissed on the bed.

⊠ ⊠ ⊠

I want to lie to you and write passionately about the horror of war, of life itself... and it would be a lie. So much is just boredom, perhaps twenty minutes in a thousand hours has the juice of existence squeezed in our veins.

If you're doing better, send me the recipe.

⊠ ⊠ ⊠

Kids and animals are the same – give them chow, a warm spot to sleep, and a wide open place to crap.

I taught my four year old simple Vietnamese phrases.

"Daddy dinky dau," she would say at the dinner table as packaged macaroni and cheese ran down her face.

"Baby Girl Number One," I'd answer.

"Beau coup Number One, Dad."

This kid of mine, call her Jennifer, came closest to seeing my ghost. Sometimes she would catch him sitting next to me, laugh, and point at him.

"Number Ten," she would say.

The old man held her hair once in his ugly brown flippers. But mainly, he ignored her.

I was his big fish
hooked in the line.

⊠ ⊠ ⊠

"Beel, you have a cigarette?" he asked.

I flipped him a Salem.

"This is a bad place," he sang, sucking in air, hot and tired.
"People turn yellow in bed."

He was referring to the vicious side effects of Thorazine

and Mellaril. Half the ward looked like dead hepatic junkies shuffling off to the med. locker for a hit.

Hell, I joined in with them.

The dead children stayed buried under the tranquilizer; psychoactive drugs are quiet reality – slow and manage-able.

"Did I kill her?" I asked the old man, who was playing with the unlit smoke.

"No… just pain."
"How about the kids?"
"No."
"Then what, huh?"
"Yourself, Beel, kill yourself."

◙ ◙ ◙

Dead faces in the wall.

I've seen them since I was a kid. I saw more than a few in an eight whore house in Can Tho.

I dream of looking at my dead face on the bedroom wall.

It ain't the prettiest.

◙ ◙ ◙

A turd hanging from her ass like a child being born.

That's my only memory of my daughter ripping her way out of my wife. No hair, no face, no weight – just my wife crapping on sterile sheets.

O yeah.

◙ ◙ ◙

The dialogue of a violent ward isn't worth repeating...
the glazed eyes of demons have no method to their
madness.

We called the nurses "whore."

They called us "such assholes."

The pack of matches hung by the nurse's station saw
more action, more goddamn life, than group therapy. We
put in time, time riding the elevator sideways through the
basement of hell, pushing all the medication buttons.
Nobody got better; we learned to cover our sickness with
the right
words.

My mother showed once to see about some money for the
kids. A manic depressive herself, none of the screaming
yellow demons phased her.

Not one bit.

❖ ❖ ❖

Some mistakes and secrets you never get past – they dog
every damn step you take, and after years of carrying
them, they don't weigh anything... but your body weight.

I tried killing myself in degrees, and failed all at once.
My life ran backwards – shooting dope on the best day of
my life, taking pictures on the worst.

Family made me uncomfortable; friends suffocated.

The first five minutes of meeting a stranger are the best. I
can actually listen to words fall out of their mouths. And
then be bored when the anonymity drops.

As the VA doctors repeatedly said, "Bill, you begin and end in Vietnam."

Naw, I just know where I'm welcome.

❖ ❖ ❖

"Hell is here," Chuck said, a finger pointed like a gun to his temple. "Don't need to die... to die, Beel."

I chewed the Salisbury steak off the patient dinner tray. The gravy had been flung onto the peas, the carrots, and a small piece of sheet cake.

"And you want me to die?" I asked.

"No. To live."

"You're saying nothing to me," I said, sopping up gravy with the vanilla cake. "I'm not looking to die, or to live."

"Then you dead," he answered me, and placed a piece of decayed flesh on my bed. "That the finger you lost in the Delta. You and it," he clasped his hands together, "are one."

The nurse nailed me with a shot.

❖ ❖ ❖

The sound of a ping pong ball against the wall.
4:15 a.m. on the Psych ward. Terror in the bed.

"That man lost his soul," Chuck commented, "and those balls aren't giving it back."

All I knew was; that twenty-six year old ex-marine was a loud pain in the ass who spit shined his civilian shoes... kind of a man who stood too close to you when he spoke.

Fuck it.

I was checking out that day with two months of VA disability checks in my pocket. I had eaten over a hundred pounds of starch.

I was gone with Chuck, and not home.

⊠ ⊠ ⊠

Three rooms if you if you count the bathroom. Roaches crawling down the kitchen walls. Spider webs around the bathroom mirror. Soiled wash and wear carpet in the living room/den/bedroom.It was furnished, right down to food encrusted utensils in a kitchen drawer. No sheets, but a blanket was left folded in the corner.

It was going to be fine, not perfect. Like a picture of the family that's in focus but the light is a bit dim to make out the grown together eyebrows.

No one came to that part of town. No one that wasn't already committed to the underbelly.

⊠ ⊠ ⊠

"Home is hell, anywhere, Beel," Chuck said as he watched me fling a full pan of boiling water against the kitchen wall, killing maybe fifty roaches.

I knew he hated the place and missed my kids… unlike me. It felt like I was sucking in air, not kids' diapers. "Careful with the glass, my man, it'll cut the hell out of your toes," I said to him, pointing at the half smashed fifth on the floor, next to a broken coffee cup.

"Don't matter."

I should've known.

And then he added, "There are quicker ways… "
(heavy silence, long long pause).

That week I taped black construction paper over the
windows.

⊠ ⊠ ⊠

A million eyes dead in kleenex.

I had just finished masturbating. Chuck had disappeared
for a bit, and I was alone. Didn't feel bad at all.

People had knocked at the door; the landlord came for
the rent; it had been a quiet week. I even began to read.
The tv was never shut off, nor was the clock radio.

Then Chuck showed up with his terribly disfigured kid.
Figure her maybe six years old, a black hole where her
chest once was… goddamn ugly beast that wouldn't stay
dead.

So. I asked.

"Why ? Who the hell is she, and (more importantly) what
the hell is she doing here, in my box?"

I wanted them both out, in the street, or on the grave.
Out. Pavement dead.

"She my daughter," he answered, "killed in Delta."

I had a feeling who killed her.

⊠ ⊠ ⊠

SON OF A BITCH

1.

I only hit my mother in the face once; it was a beginning.
My right hand dripped the blood from her nose. She just
stood there, eyes too stunned to blink, then the tears and
wails began.

My father ran down the steps and I caught his ear with
my left hand. He took his mind off my mother's pain.

The family's dog barked.

It was the day after my high school graduation.

2.

I started living in my car, a Plymouth Valiant with a slant
six motor and torn upholstery that you could've found
parked two doors down the street from my parents.

No girlfriend – I was an ugly bastard, but there were
groceries in the front seat, garbage thrown in the back. I
spent the days looking for a job, any job, and there
weren't any – or they weren't having me.

3.

I walked into the recruiter's office and signed the papers
in fifteen minutes. He took four years of my life; I took
freedom.

4.

Vietnam.

5.

Almost 19 years old and wrapped into a VA hospital bed, shitting blood & worms. My face was wrapped in a hospital towel – part of a cheekbone still oozed pus & rice paddy slime.

An old alcoholic thrashed in the bed next to me.

The night nurse caught him drinking piss out of a handheld urinal.

6.

My mother visited; the old man sent a card.

7.

I plopped a joint into the trach hole and hit on it hard – nobody shared it. The badly crippled men, quads and paras, had their own ward… and bygod they knew how to suicide like champions; I was with the run-of-the-mill gimps – burns, dead eyes, cancer and all those guys with the wicked shakes and stares.

8.

Turn the channel.
Flick an ash.
Time got time.

9.

My mother was visiting when the nurse soaked my bandages off for the first time. She puked; I was fascinated with my grotesqueness. The other guys on the ward barely noticed.

– there were uglier things.

10.

Shots came, and shots came. Young recent graduates of medical schools learned paychecks on our bodies. I itched and a shot came; I touched the hole that had been my mouth and cried. A shot slid under my skin.

I loved those shots.

11.

The alcoholic died.

I saw them wrap him up tight in plastic and move him off the ward. A young orderly, no more than a kid, wiped down the bed in disinfectant and put his personal stuff in another bag for the relatives.

Hell, there were no relatives.

12.

I woke up with a bag of Seconal tied around my eyes.

13.

The nurses and orderlies fed me a bag of food through a tube stuck through my hole, then washed it down with milk and Maalox. Breakfast, lunch, and dinner – a bag of chow.

My beard had began to stick through the bandages and curled around them like crabgrass cracking concrete.

14.

I couldn't feel my ears. They weren't attached anymore.

15.

Red Cross ladies came to the floor Thursdays with a cookie and juice cart; they were more pathetic than us, trying desperately to come to grips with their frail humanity, and failing.

A young one offered me juice but not her eyes.
It took her a full ten seconds to realize I couldn't drink it.
She never came back.

16.
I smelled the pus running down the side of my face... I was in my grave, hating every ripped inch of my body as skin fell like the very snow on my bed.

If they hadn't restrained my hands, I would've dug them straight through my face and pulled out what was left.

Nothing.

17.
After two months in a hospital bed...

I wanted to masturbate. Badly. What was beneath the gauze of my face wasn't going to be changed in a lifetime but a full prostate gland and swollen balls could be drained in a matter of eye blinks. No privacy, too much time.

Turn the tv back on.

Forget the nuts.

18.
Mother visited again, sick, paler than most of the patients. She brought a year's worth of Reader's Digests and flannel slippers.

I walked her off the ward

her hands and upper arms shaking badly.

19.
As patients, we were strangers to each other – maybe
Vietnam did that, maybe our beaten bodies did it – it
didn't matter; we slept within an arm's reach of another
man's sickness.

Men died in their beds quietly after a long sigh or a
scream, then nothing… shaming us to let ourselves live.

20.
Surgery. 49 more facial scars.

Maybe a mouth.

21.
Days passed without much pain, or thought. Chow and
doctors arrived on time; a nurse turned the lights off at 10
p.m. A window with metal grating to stare out of when
the tv ran dry.

The VA was paying me a 100% disability check each
month for a holiday in the sun. My old man was cashing
the checks and drank them down. A car was involved.

22.
An old cretin with warts for hands did the final surgery on
my face. I looked about human, with a grin that tilted
towards my right shoulder.

The left ear prosthetic was attached; the right was rebuilt
with skin from my ass.

It took me a few weeks to learn how to eat, the muscles gone in my lower jaw – food spilled like an open sack from my mouth. The trach was closed; I remembered how to talk

and hate my stupid voice.

23.
Three months later, I moved back into the family's home, right down into the basement. My bed was right next to the gas dryer. Clothes still in cardboard boxes.

I only went out at night, when the scars became shadows.

And I masturbated every day

joyfully.

24.
I paid for my first woman – a young brunette blonde in bright white boots and a yellow raincoat. I came once on her belly, once in her twat.

She reached into my pants that were laying on the floor and dug out my wallet.

I dug out her teeth.

25.
Back home, the old man left me alone and the old lady drank; it felt like the VA except the family dog stayed in the basement with me.

26.
Victims of the vampire.

I met her through my brother (she was his dealer). She
lived in a trailer parked behind her family's house; just her
and her half-black baby, alone in the worst sense. She had
great pot.

We didn't talk much, just a little tv and maybe some
cards. Got high. I always left before sunrise.

She killed herself before that baby's first birthday.

27.
A nasty habit, this carving small pieces of skin off my
body and licking the wound with my tongue. This is
fucking sick, I would say to myself as I pulled the blade
out from under the bed.

Maybe I couldn't quite believe I was human.

Maybe I liked it.

28.
Just touch them, put your finger on their back, leg, or
face, anywhere on their body but never let them feel it. I
did it to hundreds of people, strangers and friends alike,
and whispered to each and every one of them: Doom on
you.

One night I touched the clerk at the convenience store
three times right on his face and neck; he looked so hard
at my scars he never saw the finger.

My dying grandfather never felt my index finger on his
arm nor did he hear my words

I'm doomed too.

29.

I worked on my voice. I worked on my car. But mainly, I did nothing. Passed time in the basement. There were no expectations, or much thought about the future; I waited. People and situations would show up and stand in front of my body.

I waited.

30.

I carved a little more.